FOR MY CHELLA FELLAS, WiTH TWO HEAPiNG
SCOOPS OF LOVE -ARB

FOR MY LiTTLE SLiCE AND SHORT STACK,
WHOSE APPETiTE FOR ADVENTURE KNOWS
NO BOUNDS -SEO

Hi! i'M CALVIN. i LiVE iN THE UNiTED STATES, AND MY FAVORiTE FOOD iS iCE CREAM.

I COULD EAT ICE CREAM EVERY DAY. I USUALLY USE A SPOON TO EAT IT, BUT MY FAVORITE WAY TO EAT IT IS IN A WAFFLE CONE!

THIS IS MY BROTHER, CARTER. HE EATS SOME FOODS WITH HIS MOUTH, AND HE ALSO HAS A SPECIAL BUTTON IN HIS TUMMY FOR EATING. THIS IS CALLED A G TUBE.

OUR DAD MAKES SPECIAL SMOOTHIES FOR CARTER TO
HELP HIM EAT. HE USES A SYRINGE ATTACHED TO
CARTER'S G TUBE TO DELIVER FOOD INTO HIS TUMMY.

I LOVE TO HELP MAKE MY BROTHER'S SMOOTHIES (AND I ALSO LOVE SNEAKING A FEW BLUEBERRIES FOR MYSELF)!

OUR COUSIN, EVERETT, IS TWO MONTHS OLD. HE EATS FROM A BOTTLE OF FORMULA, WHICH IS MILK MADE WITH WATER AND A SPECIAL POWDER FULL OF NUTRIENTS. HE LOVES MEALTIMES!

OUR FRIEND, RUNE, IS ALSO TWO MONTHS OLD. HE LIVES IN THAILAND. HE EATS MILK FROM HIS MOTHER'S CHEST. ISN'T THAT AMAZING?

OUR FRIEND, TOBIE, LIVES IN THE PHILIPPINES. HER FAVORITE MEAL IS ADOBO, WHICH IS A DISH MADE WITH MEAT, GARLIC, SOY SAUCE, VINEGAR, BAY LEAVES, AND BLACK PEPPER.

SHE TAKES A PINCH OF RICE AND DIPS IT INTO THE STEW
TO EAT IT. IT'S SO FUN TO USE YOUR HANDS TO EAT!

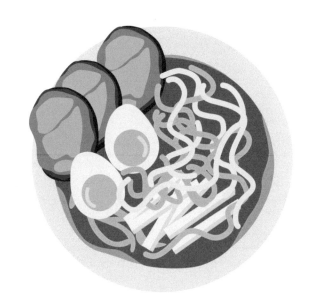

OUR FRIEND, HANA, LIVES IN JAPAN. HER FAVORITE FOOD IS RAMEN, WHICH IS A SOUP WITH LONG NOODLES, MEAT, EGGS, AND VEGETABLES.

SHE USES CHOPSTiCKS TO GRASP THE NOODLES AND A SPECiAL SPOON CALLED A "CHiRiRENGE" TO SiP THE BROTH. iT TASTES SO GOOD!

OUR FRIEND, DESTA, LIVES IN ETHIOPIA. THEIR FAMILY USES STRIPS OF A FLAT AND SPONGY BREAD CALLED INJERA TO SCOOP UP STEWS AND SALADS.

THEIR FAVORITE DISH IS MISIR WOT, A THICK STEW MADE
WITH RED LENTILS AND YUMMY SPICES. THE INJERA
SOAKS IN ALL OF THE FLAVORS OF THE STEW AND GIVES
YOU A PERFECT BITE!

OUR NEIGHBOR, EMMA, RECENTLY HAD A MEDICAL
PROCEDURE ON HER TUMMY, AND CAN'T EAT FOOD WITH
HER MOUTH WHILE SHE'S HEALING. INSTEAD, SHE USES A
TINY FLEXIBLE TUBE THAT RUNS FROM HER NOSE INTO
HER STOMACH TO EAT. THIS IS CALLED AN NG TUBE.

HER MOM MAKES HER SPECIAL SMOOTHIES TO PUT INTO HER NG TUBE. EMMA'S FAVORITE SMOOTHIE HAS OATMEAL, PEACHES, SWEET POTATO, TOFU, KEFIR, AND COCONUT OIL IN IT. HOW YUMMY!

OUR FRIEND, HARVEY, LIVES IN GERMANY. HIS FAVORITE
FOOD IS SCHNITZEL, WHICH IS A MEAT THAT HAS BEEN
FLATTENED, BREADED, AND FRIED. HIS GRANDPA SERVES
IT WITH WARM POTATO SALAD.

HE USES A KNIFE AND FORK TO CUT AND EAT IT.
SCHNITZEL IS DELICIOUS!

OUR FRIEND, DIEGO, LIVES IN VENEZUELA. HE LOVES AREPAS, WHICH ARE PANCAKE-LIKE TORTILLAS MADE WITH CORN, WATER, AND SALT.

HIS MAMA PREPARES THEM STUFFED WITH BLACK BEANS,
AVOCADO, TOMATO, MELTED CHEESE, AND ONIONS. HE
EATS THEM WITH HIS HANDS. HOW TASTY!

OUR FRIEND, GRACE, LIVES IN CANADA. SHE WAS BORN WITH A MEDICAL CONDITION CALLED CROHN'S DISEASE. THIS CAUSES IRRITATION AND PAIN IN HER DIGESTIVE SYSTEM, SO SOMETIMES SHE DOES NOT EAT ANY FOOD IN HER MOUTH OR HER TUMMY.

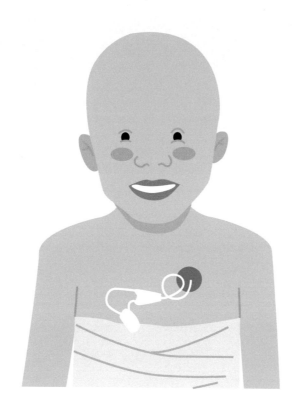

INSTEAD, SHE HAS A SPECIAL BUTTON ON HER CHEST
CALLED AN iV PORT. HER PARENTS ATTACH A TUBE TO
HER iV PORT AND GiVE HER A LiQUiD FULL OF ViTAMiNS,
MiNERALS, AND MEDiCiNE. THiS NUTRiTiOUS iV MAKES
GRACE FEEL SO MUCH BETTER!

OUR FRIEND, SAM, LIVES IN JAMAICA. DURING SPECIAL HOLIDAYS, THEIR GRANDMA MAKES FISH TEA: A SPICY SOUP MADE WITH SEAFOOD, CORN, POTATOES, CARROTS, OKRA, SPICY PEPPERS, AND HERBS.

IT'S COOKED FOR HOURS IN COCONUT MILK AND SERVED
IN STYROFOAM CUPS. HOW COOL IS THAT?!

THERE ARE SO MANY WAYS THAT WE CAN NOURISH OUR BODIES WITH HEALTHY AND HAPPY FOODS.

WHICH ONE iS YOUR FAVORiTE?

RECIPES THAT NOURISH

CARTER'S SMOOTHIE
THE PERFECT SNICKERDOODLE SNACK!

- 1/2 AVOCADO
- 1 FROZEN BANANA
- 2 TBSP PEANUT OR CASHEW BUTTER
- 1 SCOOP VANILLA PROTEIN POWDER
- 2 HANDFULS OF BABY SPINACH
- 1 CUP ALMOND MILK, MORE IF NEEDED FOR PROPER TEXTURE
- 1 TSP CINNAMON

DIRECTIONS

1. ADD ALL TO BLENDER
2. BLEND UNTIL IT IS YOUR DESIRED CONSISTENCY (THIN WITH ADDITIONAL ALMOND MILK IF PREPARING FOR CONSUMPTION THROUGH A G TUBE)
3. ENJOY VIA G TUBE OR WITH A STRAW, IT'S DELICIOUS EITHER WAY!

TOBIE'S ADOBO

- 2 POUNDS BONELESS PORK COUNTRY RIBS, CUBED
- 1 MEDIUM WHITE ONION, DICED
- 1 HEAD GARLIC, MINCED
- 4 TABLESPOONS WHITE OR APPLE CIDER VINEGAR
- 1/2 CUP SOY SAUCE
- 1 TABLESPOON GROUND BLACK PEPPER
- 1 TABLESPOON COCONUT SUGAR
- 5 BAY LEAVES
- 3 STALKS GREEN ONION, CHOPPED

DIRECTIONS

1. MARINATE THE CUBED PORK IN A MIXTURE OF SOY SAUCE, VINEGAR, GARLIC, ONIONS, BLACK PEPPER, AND SUGAR FOR AT LEAST ONE HOUR (ALTHOUGH OVERNIGHT IS PREFERABLE)
2. REMOVE PORK FROM MARINADE AND RESERVE MARINADE FOR LATER
3. BROWN PORK CUBES ON ALL SIDES IN A POT OR INSTANT POT
4. ADD LEFTOVER MARINADE, TWO CUPS OF WATER, AND BAY LEAVES TO POT
5. PRESSURE COOK THE STEW FOR 20 MINUTES OR SIMMER ON STOVETOP FOR ONE HOUR (ADDING WATER IF NECESSARY TO DESIRED CONSISTENCY)
6. GARNISH WITH CHOPPED GREEN ONION AND SERVE WITH RICE
7. ENJOY!

HANA'S RAMEN

- 1 LB PORK BELLY
- SALT
- 8 CUPS WATER
- 3 TABLESPOONS APPLE CIDER VINEGAR
- 1 KNOB GINGER
- 4 CLOVES GARLIC
- 3 STALKS GREEN ONION
- RAMEN NOODLES
- SOFT BOILED EGG
- SPINACH
- CANNED BAMBOO SHOOTS
- 1 TEASPOON SESAME OIL
- 1 SHEET FURIKAKE (DRIED SEAWEED

DIRECTIONS

1. RUB SALT ALL OVER PORK BELLY AND LEAVE IN FRIDGE FOR AT LEAST TWO HOURS
2. ADD THE SALTED PORK, WATER, VINEGAR, SLICED GINGER, SLICED GARLIC, AND THE WHITES OF THE GREEN ONION (SLICED) TO AN INSTANT POT OR STOCK POT
3. PRESSURE COOK THE MIXTURE FOR 20 MINUTES ON HIGH WITH A NATURAL RELEASE OR SIMMER ON STOVETOP FOR TWO HOURS
4. REMOVE PORK AND LET COOL BEFORE SLICING THINLY
5. IN THE MEANTIME, SOFT BOIL ONE EGG IN SEPARATE POT; PREPARE RAMEN NOODLES ACCORDING TO THE PACKAGE DIRECTIONS DIRECTLY IN THE SOUP
6. WILT THE SPINACH AND WARM THE CANNED BAMBOO SHOOTS IN THE SOUP TOWARDS THE END OF THE RAMEN COOKING TIME
7. SERVE RAMEN NOODLES WITH BROTH, SPINACH, BAMBOO SHOOTS, AND SOFT BOILED EGG SLICED IN HALF, TOPPED WITH A DRIZZLE OF SESAME OIL AND A PINCH OF DRIED SEAWEED
8. ENJOY!

DESTA'S INJERA

LIKE SOURDOUGH BREAD, TRADITIONAL INJERA REQUIRES A STARTER (CALLED "ERSHO"). THIS IS TYPICALLY MADE ABOUT THREE DAYS IN ADVANCE OF MAKING THE INJERA. IF AFTER TWO DAYS, YOUR STARTER IS NOT BEGINNING TO BUBBLE, YOU CAN ADD 1 TEASPOON OF YEAST AND WAIT UNTIL THE BUBBLING BEGINS.

- 1 CUP TEFF FLOUR
- 2 CUPS ROOM TEMPERATURE WATER
- 1 TSP SALT
- 2 TABLESPOONS OIL

DIRECTIONS

1. COMBINE TEFF AND WATER THOROUGHLY IN A MASON JAR, ENSURING THERE ARE NO LUMPS, AND COVER LOOSELY WITH A KITCHEN TOWEL
2. ALLOW TO FERMENT FOR THREE DAYS
3. ONCE BUBBLING, REMOVE FROM THE JAR AND PLACE IN MIXING BOWL
4. ADD SALT AND STIR THOROUGHLY
5. HEAT A NONSTICK PAN OR SKILLET ON HIGH HEAT AND ADD OIL
6. POUR A THIN LAYER OF BATTER INTO THE SKILLET (THICKER THAN A CREPE BUT THINNER THAN A PANCAKE)
7. COOK ONE ON SIDE UNTIL BUBBLES APPEAR ACROSS THE TOP, APPROXIMATELY 1.5 TO 2 MINUTES
8. REMOVE FROM HEAT AND COOL
9. RIP INTO STRIPS AND ENJOY!

HARVEY'S SCHNITZEL

- 2 CHICKEN BREASTS
- 1/2 CUP FLOUR
- 2 EGGS
- 1/4 CUP MILK
- 1 CUP MATZO MEAL OR BREADCRUMBS
- 1/4 TEASPOON PAPRIKA
- 1/4 TEASPOON GROUND BLACK PEPPER
- 1/4 TEASPOON SALT
- OIL FOR FRYING
- LEMON WEDGES
- PARSLEY

DIRECTIONS

1. CAREFULLY BUTTERFLY EACH CHICKEN BREAST
2. USE A MEAT TENDERIZER TO POUND THE CHICKEN INTO A THIN PATTY
3. PLACE FLOUR IN A SEPARATE BOWL OR PLASTIC GALLON BAG
4. USE A FORK TO WHISK EGGS AND MILK IN A BOWL
5. COMBINE MATZO MEAL OR BREADCRUMBS WITH PAPRIKA, THYME, PEPPER, AND SALT
6. DREDGE EACH CHICKEN BREAST THROUGH FLOUR
7. DIP FLOURED CHICKEN BREASTS IN THE EGG AND MILK MIXTURE
8. DREDGE CHICKEN BREASTS THROUGH THE MATZO MEAL OR BREADCRUMB MIXTURE AND SHAKE OFF EXCESS BREADING
9. IN A SKILLET, FRY CHICKEN TO GOLDEN BROWN ON EACH SIDE
10. SERVE SCHNITZEL HOT WITH LEMON WEDGES AND A SPRINKLE OF FRESH PARSLEY AND ENJOY!

DIEGO'S AREPAS

- 2 CUPS PRE-COOKED WHITE CORN MEAL
- 2.5 CUPS WATER
- 1 TEASPOON SALT
- 2 TABLESPOONS OIL TO BRUSH THE AREPAS BEFORE COOKING

DIRECTIONS

FOR THE DOUGH

1. STIR TOGETHER THE CORN MEAL AND SALT
2. GRADUALLY ADD THE WATER, AND MIX BY HAND FOR TWO MINUTES
3. LET REST FOR FIVE MINUTES

TO ASSEMBLE AREPAS

1. DIVIDE THE DOUGH INTO 8-10 EQUAL-SIZED PORTIONS
2. SHAPE THE DOUGH INTO BALLS, THEN FLATTEN INTO 4-5 INCH ROUNDS IN THE PALM OF YOUR HAND
3. BRUSH OR SPRAY OIL INTO AN EVEN LAYER ALL OVER THE AREPAS
4. PLACE INTO THE AIR FRYER AND COOK FOR 10 MINUTES AT 390°F
5. ALTERNATIVELY, YOU CAN DEEP FRY OR PAN FRY THE AREPAS INSTEAD
6. SLICE AND FILL THEM WITH DIEGO'S FAVORITES (BLACK BEANS, AVOCADO, MELTED CHEESE, AND ONIONS) OR WITH YOUR OWN CREATION AND ENJOY!

SAM'S FISH TEA

Ingredients

- 2 TABLESPOONS OiL
- HALF YELLOW ONiON, CHOPPED
- 6 SPRiGS THYME, MiNCED
- FULL HEAD OF GARLiC, CHOPPED
- 8 CUPS FiSH STOCK
- 1 TSP WHOLE ALLSPiCE
- 2 CORN COBS, SLiCED iNTO ROUNDS
- SMALL BAG OF BABY DUTCH POTATOES
- HANDFUL OF OKRA, SLiCED
- 2 CARROTS, CHOPPED
- 1 POUND SHRiMP
- 1 POUND FiSH OF CHOiCE, CUT iNTO 2-iNCH CHUNKS
- 1 SMALL SCOTCH BONNET PEPPER

DIRECTIONS

1. TURN iNSTANT POT TO "SAUTE" MODE AND ADD OiL
2. ONCE HOT, ADD ONiONS AND THYME, STiRRiNG OCCASiONAL TO PREVENT STiCKiNG
3. WHEN ONiONS BECOME TRANSLUCENT, ADD GARLiC AND CONTINUE SAUTEiNG FOR 5 MiNUTES
4. TURN OFF SAUTE FUNCTiON AND ADD ALLSPiCE, CORN, POTATOES, OKRA, CARROTS, AND FiSH STOCK TO THE POT
5. COVER AND TURN VENTiNG KNOB TO "SEALiNG"
6. MANUALLY PRESSURE COOK ON HiGH FOR 8 MINUTES TO SOFTEN THE VEGETABLES
7. MANUALLY RELEASE THE STEAM AND REMOVE LiD WHEN COMPLETELY VENTED
8. TURN ON SAUTE MODE AND ADD SHRiMP, FiSH, AND SCOTCH BONNET PEPPER
9. SAUTE FOR FiVE MiNUTES OR UNTiL COOKED, AND GENTLY REMOVE SCOTCH BONNET PEPPER (SO AS NOT TO BREAK iT AND RELEASE TOO MUCH HEAT)
10. GARNiSH WiTH CHOPPED SCALLiONS OR CiLANTRO AND ENjOY!

ASHLEY BURKMAN, ND

ASHLEY IS A LICENSED NATUROPATHIC DOCTOR (CONNECTICUT) AND WAHL'S PROTOCOL ® CERTIFIED HEALTH PROFESSIONAL (A CERTIFICATION THAT DESIGNATES ADDITIONAL TRAINING IN DIET THERAPY GEARED TOWARD THOSE WHO SUFFER AUTOIMMUNE OR OTHER CHRONIC ILLNESSES). AN IOWA NATIVE, SHE ENJOYS SPENDING TIME WITH FRIENDS AND FAMILY, SEARCHING FOR NEW HIKING TRAILS TO CONQUER, AND WATCHING COMEDY SHOWS EVERY CHANCE SHE GETS. SHE IS PRIVILEGED TO WATCH THE TWO LIGHTS OF HER LIFE, TWINS CALVIN AND CARTER, GROW!

LEARN MORE ABOUT HER AT GOODHABITSND.COM

SARAH OUANO, ND

SARAH IS A LICENSED NATUROPATHIC DOCTOR (VERMONT), CERTIFIED LACTATION SUPPORT COUNSELOR, AND AUTHOR OF SEVERAL HEALTH-BASED CHILDREN'S BOOKS, COOKBOOKS, AND MEDICAL TEXTS. SHE IS PASSIONATE ABOUT SOCIAL JUSTICE AND HEALTHCARE, PARTICULARLY IN THE REALM OF FOOD SECURITY AND ACCESS. SHE LOVES NOODLES, HER TYPEWRITER, THRIFTING, MUSICAL THEATRE, HER HOME STATE OF CALIFORNIA, ALLIE, TOBIE, JAMES, ELPHIE, AND VESPA VERY MUCH.

LEARN MORE ABOUT HER AT MSHA.KE/NATUROPROJECTS

Made in the USA
Columbia, SC
21 November 2024

47196995R00024